By Tl
Twenty-Five Years of
Pastoring Black Baptists

GOD BLESS
PAS. BOULWARE, SR.
R. Bu
11/2/19

Dr. Robert E. Baines, Jr.

By The Grace of God: Twenty-Five Years of Pastoring Black Baptists

Visit the author's websites at
www.RobertBaines.com
Disclaimer

Although every attempt has been made to produce the most accurate and trustworthy information possible, Robert E. Baines, Jr. does not accept liability for any actions taken as a result of reading this publication. This publication is not intended as counseling.

Your Free Gift

I have **a free gift for** you. It is my way of saying **"Thank You"** for supporting my writing ministry. I wrote a booklet entitled, *"Inspiration From Psalm 23."* The booklet contains six encouraging devotionals based on Psalm 23. All you have to do is click the link below and then supply your name and email, in exchange for the booklet, which will be emailed to you in pdf format.

www.RobertBaines.com

Dedication and Acknowledgement

This book is dedicated to all of those who see anything admirable in my life. I want you to know that it is God's grace, not my goodness or kindness. I am indebted to my wife and Sis. Gerri Sanders for helping with the proofreading. I am thankful to Southern Baptist Church in Cincinnati, Ohio for allowing me the freedom to be able to further my writing ministry.

Table of Content

Introduction

The purpose of this book is to share some selected autobiographical reflections that underscore how gracious God has been to me with the hope that others will be inspired to trust God to work through them as well. This book also contains a number of lessons learned and convictions that I want to leave on record for especially those who have sat under my ministry and for my colleagues in ministry.

It is my hope that people will read this book and understand that what God has done and is doing in my life can be done in their lives and at much higher levels. I also pray that more Pastors would write about their life stories, lessons learned, and convictions, so that their peers and generations to come may benefit from them.

Chapter One: My Early Years

It would be such a huge mistake to think that my life has always been the way that it is today. In this chapter, I present selected memories and reflections regarding my extended family, my life up to joining the United States Air Force, return back to Buffalo, New York, and key lessons I've learned.

Extended Family

My grandparents on my father's side were Cleveland and Rebecca Baines. I remember my grandmother as being a church going woman who loved her family. She sung in the choir (i.e., Zion Missionary Baptist Church, in Buffalo, New York, where my father was the Pastor), watched over me as I played in the playground, in front of her house, and was known for enjoying life. My grandfather was a large dark man who loved to fish with his grandchildren. I remember catching worms and fishing with him on his blue boat. I also remember him killing a pig for Christmas and having a house full of family members. He was not much of a church-goer around me. On my father's side, there were 13 uncles, two aunts, and a host of cousins and friends of the family.

My grandparents on my mother's side were Mack and Virgie Young. My grandmother was a saintly woman at church (i.e., Antioch Fire Baptized Holiness Church in Buffalo, New York) and hard worker at home (i.e., she made pie crust for my uncle's restaurant). I remember her watching over me from time to time, as I played in the nearby neighborhood. My grandfather and grandmother were separated all of my life. I remember my grandfather as short and stocky. He did not have the best reputation as a family man. I don't remember him being much of a church-goer. On my mother's side were five uncles, nine aunts, and host of cousins and friends of the family.

I am thankful that I learned from my extended family that there are all kinds of personality types in a family, and love can cover a multitude of sins. Love can override substance abuse, domestic violence, sexual preferences, lack of church, classism, and other issues.

Parents

I was born to Robert and Ruby Baines on Tuesday, September 6, 1966, in Buffalo, New York. My dad worked hard to make a living. I remember him going to work in an automobile plant (i.e., Chevrolet) before the sun came up and coming back home after the sun had went down. He became a journeyman electrician, but left the plant to Pastor the Zion Missionary Baptist Church, in Buffalo, New York. From the humble beginnings of living in a small attached parsonage that he had to renovate with his own hands, he was able to lead the church in building two well respected church buildings. I have written a book about my father, who was one of my heroes - *From Skippers, Virginia to Eternal Life: A Salute to Rev. Dr. Robert E. Baines, Sr. and Lessons for Those Yet on the Journey* (Amazon.com, 2012). He died of cancer on my 45th birthday in 2011.

My mother, who is still alive at the time of this writing, was a homemaker, during my earliest years. I remember her working with my grandmother to make pie crust for my uncle's restaurant from time to time. She has always been a regular in church and even more so as a Pastor's wife.

My parents separated, when I was nine years old. They later divorced, and my father remarried, after a number of years. I remember how their marriage was not working for them, even though they both loved my sister (i.e., Robin S. Baines, M.D.) and me. With marital separation came the issues of my mother having to find work, public assistance, and visitation rights.

These years and memories help me to be sensitive to how fragile marriages and finances can be. I thank God for the work ethic instilled in me by especially my father, the love of the church instilled in me by both parents, and the model of parental love for my children inspired by them.

From Early Push to the United States Air Force

I don't really remember being in Early Push, I think they call it Head Start now (i.e., a pre-school program for children who may need some school readiness preparation), but my mother told me that I went. I do remember going to St. Ann's Catholic School and being deliberately transferred to Public School #64 because of some behavioral problems. After my father's whipping me, I don't think I had another behavioral problem in school (smile).

I did well in elementary school. Math was my favorite subject. I don't remember any affection for history or English. I don't remember any career aspirations other than something that provided a comfortable living.

Around the age of 10 years old, I recall accepting Jesus as my savior by faith. I believe it was a Thursday night, during a revival, at the Antioch Fire Baptized Holiness Church, in Buffalo, New York. I recall my grandmother, Mother Young, and one of the other Mothers, Mother White, praying with me at what we called the altar (i.e., the prayer rail near the pulpit podium). From the mourner's bench (i.e., front pew) I went to the prayer rail, after the female minister had preached. The Mothers coached me in saying, "save me Jesus, save me Lord"! After a while, "save me Jesus" became "thank You Jesus, thank You Lord!" It was a euphoric experience. You would have had to have been there to understand why this memory is so precious to me.

The building is gone, but my mother is still a member of this church. It is interesting that my father accepted Jesus in the same church under the ministry of Elder M. L. Bowman. Elder Bowman's son is now the Pastor - Bishop James Bowman.

Around the age of 12, I decided to be baptized by my father and Pastor, at the Zion Missionary Baptist Church. I'm thankful that my parents allowed me to discern and follow God's will for my life.

I remember shoveling snow in Buffalo, New York, as a child, as well as working for my Uncle Paul, in his restaurant for extra money. It was during my snow shoveling years (i.e., around 12 years old) that I began to tithe on whatever money I received.

I was an honor graduate from Hutchinson Central Technical High School (i.e., Hutch Tech), in computer electronics. I played football and ran track for one year, my senior year. My father would not let me do much until I got on the honor roll.

During my high school years, I went to live with my father. In his attempts to make a man out of me, I remember having to work in a corner store that he owned for $2 an hour on the weekends and being the janitor at the church for about $20 a week. I had to shop at Goodwill and live in an attic that had a hole in the ceiling. It took quite a while to find a rationale for the Pastor's son (i.e., me) having to go through this. What I know for a fact is that I can appreciate where I am and what I have now, because I know what it is to not have much.

I don't think I was as hard on my children, but I did help them understand that my socio-economic status was not theirs. They had to go out and earn their socio-economic status, as an adult.

Even though I was a poor, minority, scholar, athlete, I yet ended up in the Air Force commissary (i.e., military grocery store), receiving trucks, stocking shelves, and even ringing a cash register. I joined the Air Force because I saw it as a solid way to get a job, pay for my education, and cast my own shadow. I also liked the uniform (smile). The Marine uniform was nice, but I feared that I would be on the front line of a war, if I joined the Marines.

There is a part of me that wish I had received better guidance in high school. As a poor Black male with honor roll grades, I could have received enough scholarship money to do something in the field of computer electronics or engineering. However, if I had gone that way then maybe I would have been tempted to do that more than obey God's calling for me to be a Pastor. Who knows?

1984

I accepted the call to preach the Gospel around June 1984, after I had committed to joining the Air Force. I did not have any extra ordinary event to happen in life. I simply had and still have a burning desire to preach the word of God. I preached my initial sermon in the last quarter of 1984.

I went to basic training for the Air Force as close to my high school graduation as possible, in July 1984. Imagine my being raised in Buffalo, New York but now wearing long sleeved shirts, combat boots, and a cap in the San Antonio, Texas area during the months of July and August. Can you say hhhot!!! I have no regrets about the military. It was good character building and a nice break from being in Buffalo, New York.

On December 31, 1984, I married my high school sweet heart, Daphene Tucker, in a Watch Night Service. We got into a very used car that was given to me by my father and drove from Buffalo, New York to the Washington D. C. area about 72 hours after we were married. This was my first car and my first rode trip by myself. Daphene did not know how to drive. The car broke down on the way. We spent most of the little money that we had fixing up that piece of a car and getting to Andrews Air Force Base (i.e., outside of Washington, D.C.).

We got married because we were two Christians who were in love and believed that we could make a life together. We were trusting God to honor our faith in His teaching that "it was better to marry than to burn" (i.e., we wanted to sanctify our sexual attraction to each other). The original plan was to wait until we were 25 years old with college degrees and jobs. But 500 miles between us and strong "desires" moved us to plan B - getting married at 18 years old.

My mother-in-law, Beatrice Tucker, thought that I had gotten her daughter pregnant and that I was trying to do the right thing. My father told me that he would rather walk behind my casket than to be a part of my marrying Daphene. He tried hard to talk her out of marrying me. When he saw that we were going to get married anyway, he reluctantly cooperated. His comment grew from the pain that he experienced in going through a divorce and his thinking that we were not ready for marriage. He grew to admire our love and marriage.

1984 was quite a year. I graduated from high school, accepted the call to preach, joined the Air Force, got married at 18 years old to an 18 year old, and was on my way to relocating my wife 500 miles away from anyone we knew. Only the Lord could kept us.

The Air Force

I served for four years in the Air Force (i.e., 1984-1988). I did my basic training at Lackland Air Force Base, near San Antonio, Texas and was then stationed at Andrews Air Force Base, near Washington D. C. for all four years. I worked in a commissary, which was essentially a military grocery store. We purchased (i.e., with my father's financial backing) and lived in a trailer on the base for about 2 ½ years. We lost money on the sell; however, we sold it because my father told us there were no trailer parks around Buffalo. We found out there were trailer parks, after the deal was done.

As I look back over this four year period, I can see the hand of the Lord. I did not find my military work very challenging. I did what I was told and could have gone up the ladder in the commissary or changed my career path. But the dissatisfaction with military work made focusing on my ministry easy.

I applied my self and earned my Associates Degree in Business Management, after changing from my initial accounting major. Even though my wife worked at various jobs and went to school to work towards her Associates Degree in Early Childhood Education, I felt a need to do extra work, so we could have a little extra financial breathing room with the birth of our first child - Daphene Latrice (i.e., named after her mother). "Daphene L" as we have grown to call her was born on May 11, 1987 - about 2 ½ years after Daphene and I were married.

While my wife worked as a restaurant server, childcare worker, and then as a clerical worker for the Environmental Protection Agency, I worked in a number of capacities as well. I bagged groceries for tips, washed dishes in the dining hall, served as a janitor at a movie theater, and sold insurance products to add to my military income. My wife and I remember walking through the frozen food section of the grocery stores to stay cool in the summer. We did not have any air conditioning in our apartment nor car, while it was 90+ degrees outside.

As an aside, I remember how my wife and I were exercising our faith in God. We were sending the tithes on what little money we were making back to Buffalo, New York, while we were looking for a church in the Maryland area. One day, we sent our check off, even though we really needed the money. The stamp fell off and the check came back to our apartment. We really needed the money then, but we re-mailed it in faith. We can both declare that God has been so faithful.

I met preacher friends during this period whom I still interact with (esp., Dr. Clevester O. Wimbish and Rev. Charlie Wimbish). I am thankful for lessons learned from Pastor Carrie Pointer at Mt. Joy Missionary Baptist Church in South East Washington D.C., Pastor Campbell at Ascension Missionary Baptist Church in Maryland, and I may never forget the love I received from Pastor Chester McDonald, Sr. at Maple Springs Baptist Church in Maryland. During this period, I would come back to Buffalo, New York about three times a year and often preached for my father.

Back to Buffalo, New York

After my tour in the military, my wife and I worked odd jobs for less than a year, before we came back to Buffalo, New York to work in a corner grocery store that my father set up for us. We named the store "D and E Market," after Daphene and Eric (i.e., my middle name is Eric). We worked in that store from about 7 a.m. to about 11 p.m., Monday through Saturday. We had a small apartment in the back of the store and two apartments that we never got around to fixing up and renting above the store. The store did not prove to be profitable.

But we took this time to further our education. I worked on my Bachelors of Science in Community and Human Services. Daphene took courses towards her Associates degree. The Lord opened up preaching opportunities, primarily through my father's relationships with local clergy. Our second and last child was born, while we lived in the apartment behind the store - Desiraye Lashanta. "Ray" as we came to know her was born on June 22, 1989. I also earned my ordination certificate in 1988.

When I saw that the store was not working, I worked where I could. I managed a little bit larger store for a company. I worked in a larger grocery store. I drove a cab (i.e., my father gave me money to try this out). And then I finally started doing something that I halfway enjoyed. I worked for an agency that helped parents get themselves together to receive their children back from foster care. I worked with a job training and homeless prevention program at the Community Action Agency.

Daphene went from working at the store to working in a childcare center. I am so thankful for my wife. It took a great deal of faith on her part to put her dreams on hold to support my dreams, but I think we can see today that it has worked out. I remember that we ran out of room in our truck, when we were moving from Maryland to Buffalo. We had to leave some of her college books and papers behind. We didn't have enough sense to simply mail the stuff to Buffalo.

Key Lessons From the Early Years

The following are some of the key lessons that I learned from my early years:

1. God can take you from humble beginnings to greater heights. I don't know of anyone who believed that the child playing in the ghetto called the Fruit Belt of Buffalo, New York would be Pastoring a prominent church in Cincinnati, Ohio with a Doctorate degree and various other blessings. In fact, I remember my elementary school principal telling me that I would mess up my life. In spite of the violence that I witnessed as a child, low income, fractured family, and feeling a little less than others,

God has done great things in and through my life.

2. Life is not easy, but with smart and hard work, you can make it. These years were known for high faith and work but low income. But by the grace of God, my faith has matured, my work is more efficient, and my wife and I are doing quite well. Anyone who looks at me now needs to remember that I bagged groceries, swept and mopped floors, cleaned toilets, drove piece of junk cars that left my wife and I stranded on a number of occasions, shopped at Goodwill and thrift stores, and the like.

3. You are not your stuff. From my humble beginnings to now, I have learned that the stuff that I possess doesn't make or break me. I was a child of God, when I was walking and catching the bus. I was a man when I was driving a cab to keep food on our table. I was a preacher before I had a Pastoral anniversary. And when my Pastoral career is over, I will still be a saved man whom God called to preach.

Chapter Two: Mt. Moriah Missionary Baptist Church

From my early years, I present my memories and reflections regarding my Pastoring the Mt. Moriah Missionary Baptist Church, in Buffalo, New York. When I came back to Buffalo from the Air Force to run a corner grocery store, I was faithful in serving at the Zion Missionary Baptist Church, where my father served as the Pastor. I was in charge of the Sunday School, preached at Zion or one of the local churches at least monthly, and worked in human services, after working in grocery stores, parking cars, and driving a cab.

I heard about Mt. Moriah being without a Pastor, so I sent in my resume. They invited me to preach. I may have preached a couple of times and they invited me to be their Pastor, in early 1990. It was a small church of about 30 people on Sunday morning, but I was under the impression that they wanted to grow. I knew that I wanted to lead them in growing.

It would be helpful to remember that I had served at a small church (Ascension Missionary Baptist Church in Maryland), two medium size churches (Mt. Joy Baptist Church in Washington, DC and Zion Missionary Baptist Church in Buffalo, New York), and a larger church (Maple Springs Baptist Church in Maryland - 600+ members in both worship services together). I read a great deal but had very little formal training. I had taken some classes at Washington Bible College, had an Associate's Degree in Business Management, and was working on my Bachelor's Degree in Community and Human Services.

From 1990 to 1991, the Lord blessed this ministry. Over 60 membership candidates were received. The number of disciples (i.e., those who study, serve, and give) grew. Several ministries were added such as Community Evangelism, Men Ministry, and Youth Ministry. The worship attendance grew from about 30 people to about 60 people. The revenue grew from about $300/week to about $630/week. A Bible based constitution and a budget/voucher system were implemented. Several improvements were made to the facilities - roof, siding, and more. In 1991, the church had over $6,000 more assets (i.e., from about $2,000 to $8,000 in the bank) than it had in 1989.

Memories and Reflections

Installation at Zion. I remember that my installation service was held at Zion Missionary Baptist Church, which was about two miles from Mt. Moriah Missionary Baptist Church. The reason for having the service at Zion was because the crowd from Zion would have been too large for the seating capacity at Mt. Moriah, not to mention the members from Mt. Moriah and others in the community. The worship service went well, as I recall. However, I made a remark about taking the reigns of the church that my one and only Deacon remembered and reminded me of. In retrospect, I may have talked with some of the officers, instead of simply declaring the location of the service.

$100/week. I started my Pastoral career receiving $100/week from about 30 members on Sunday morning. Pastor Benson had Alzheimer's diseases, which led to him becoming the emeritized Pastor. He was receiving $100/week as well. My compensation was fine with me. I was still working. And I was glad to have started my Pastoral journey at the age of 23 years old.

We started off with the understanding that "as the church grew, the Pastor would grow." The church quickly grew from $300/week revenue to about $630/week. I remember having a formula in my head of the Pastor receiving 1/3 of the church's revenue, until the compensation package was able to sustain full time employment. It was my thinking that if the church paid the Pastor 1/3 of the revenue then the Pastor could never be a burden to the church.

I asked the church for both a raise and adoption of a policy based on the formula. The wife of the only Deacon that we had agreed that I deserved the raise, but rejected the policy idea on the grounds that it was like working on commission. So she made a motion to raise my salary up to $200/week, instead of $220/week, so it would not be a commission.

I feel good about my transparency. I feel good about a 100% raise in less than a year.

But it taught me how people will try to hurt you on the bases of their beliefs. She believed that commissions were wrong and used her influence to lower my proposed raise. The idea of paying the Pastor based on church revenue is still one of my strong principles.

The Emeritized Pastor. Pastor Benson had Alzheimer's disease for my two years of Pastoring the church. He had the disease for the entire two or three years of the Pastoralship of the Pastor right before me. I am not sure what he did outside of founding and Pastoring Mt. Moriah. I do remember that it was understood that if he died, the church would continue to pay his wife the $100/week, until she died.

This situation inspires my insistence on having long term disability insurance today. If I become unable to serve, I will not be at the mercy of a church meeting. And at my demise, my wife will not have to stay at the church that I used to Pastor, so she can get a check from the church.

The leaking roof. It is a little funny today, but it was far from funny, when I was living through it. The church building was a two-story building with a flat roof. The roof was leaking, which resulted in rainwater coming through the roof and second floor ceiling, the floor of the second floor, the ceiling of the first floor, and finally into a bucket in the first floor sanctuary. When it rained on Sunday, you could hear rainwater being caught in buckets and pots in the sanctuary.

It seemed good to me to use some of the $6,000 that we had put in the bank during my approximately 18 months at the church to fix the roof. I remember the Trustees being slow in getting bids, so I just went to the yellow pages to see what could be found. One contractor gave a bid of about $1,500 and the high bid was about $4,500. The Trustees voted against fixing the roof and urged the members to do the same. They accused me of wanting to turn Mt. Moriah into a Zion. I remember one of the Trustees (Sis. R.) saying that they were used to their buckets and pots. They then discredited the low bid contractor with no alternative. The church sided with the Trustees at two different meetings. In the meantime, a section of the sheet rock ceiling fell down on the second floor. I was accused of knocking the section down to further my agenda.

At the third meeting, after I called all 75 names on my membership roster and asked them to come to the meeting and vote to the fix the roof, I finally won the vote to fix the roof. The vote was about 15 to 10, most of the people said they did not want to get involved.

In retrospect, I wrongly assumed that officers loved God and His church enough to always do what was best for the church, even if the Pastor did not make them feel like they were very important. I really believe they wanted to be treated as if they were more important than I was treating them and consequently, they held hostage their cooperation. I even remember one of the Trustees commenting that he did not appreciate me reviewing the church's financial records, even though there was rarely a week of error free transactions and record keeping.

Minutes. I remember the Church Clerk editorializing the minutes. On one occasion, she put in the minutes that the Pastor rudely said something to one of the members. Matters that had been agreed upon were omitted from the minutes. And she had recollections of matters that I did not remember taking place.

This taught me to require all minutes to be typed and submitted for my review within seven days after the meeting. All minutes are to be a record of primarily what was agreed upon, if anything. The matters that I bring to the church are normally spelled out in writing for the church's review. Thus, the minutes often say the church agreed to the attached, so we can get the exact wording of what was presented and agreed upon. The recorder and I sign off on the minutes, after we are in agreement, and these are the minutes read at the meeting for adoption. There have also been times when I have brought a tape recorder to meetings to help end debates about what was said and not said in the meeting. I did not learn these items in seminary.

Heckled by Sis. R. and Bro. R.'s repentance *(In Black Baptist Churches it is not strange to hear men referred to as Brothers and women as Sisters. The abbreviation used in this document for these terms are Bro. and Sis. The abbreviation for Deacon is Dea. and for Pastor is Pas.).* I remember Sis. R. heckling me on Sunday morning. She did not like whatever I was talking about and essentially said that is not in the Bible. I kept on preaching. I remember her singing or doing something that was out of order. I turned the microphone off on her. She hollered out that her microphone was off. I kept on preaching.

These things made me strong. Maybe a year before this writing, a member of the church that I Pastor now tried to heckle me. She essentially said that she was *not* giving and it doesn't bother her. I commented on how ignorant her pride was, called her name, and said that I am going to win this contest for the last word. She quieted down, as did those who witnessed the exchange.

I also remember a man that I am calling Bro. R. He was the musician when I got to Mt. Moriah. As I recall, I was talking to the choir in a special choir meeting. He approached me from behind to speak. I had no sense of being in danger. However, members of the church thought that I was. They stood up and got between the two of us.

After consulting with the senior officers, I presented the matter to the church. I told them that I didn't feel as if I was in danger, but if you all know otherwise then discipline was in order. It was moved and seconded to remove him from his job and church membership. In retrospect, there was bad blood between Bro. R. and the senior officers.

Maybe a year after this event, Bro. R. picked my wife and me up and drove us to Niagara Falls, Canada. There he paid for a $200 meal and drove us back home, as his way of saying that there were no hard feelings between him and me. He never came back to the church, but I saw him a couple of times outside of the church.

This taught me that God will make your enemies into those who serve you at the table of favor. God will keep you from seeing some dangers. And God will work all things out for the good of His people, if His people would simply walk by faith.

Evangelism. As a youth worker and then an Associate Minister at especially Zion and Ascension Missionary Baptist Church, I was familiar with community evangelism. So it seemed good to me to do some community evangelism to help grow the membership of the church. I remember passing out literature that invited people to the church, having community events at the church, and having evangelistic services. In fact, I preached the evangelistic services because we did not have enough money to give to those I would have wanted to come and preach for us.

The Lord blessed and over 60 people came to join or be reinstated in the church, during my time at Mt. Moriah. However, I also remember that one of the ladies who joined the church was a former member of Zion and she felt comfortable talking with me about her interactions with the other members at Mt. Moriah. She told me that the Sunday that she joined, the Church Clerk called her and told her that she did not need to be a part of Mt. Moriah. The Clerk proceeded to talk me down and discourage the young lady. As I recall, the young lady came from time to time but did not really get involved.

I remember a member or two asking me, why am I bringing all of these people into "their church." This taught me that people can run members away faster than the Pastor can bring them in. I believe that effective evangelism must not only help people accept Christ as savior by faith and normally join church, but there must be a system of supportive and encouraging relationships to help the new members stay and grow.

No preach - no pay and smoke rings. There was a Sunday in which I was invited to preach at a church in Rochester, New York. I had a local ordained minister to come and fill in for me. He was to receive a love offering, as his honorarium. When I came back, I inquired about how much was collected for him. If it was short, I was going to make up the difference.

To my surprise, the Trustees had decided that since I did not preach, I would not receive my salary for that week. This was the first Sunday that I had taken off in about 15 months, and they knew in advance that I was going to be gone. I took the Deacon up stairs to where the Trustees were meeting. I remember that demonic Sis. R. was smoking and blowing smoke rings under the "No

Smoking" sign, in the church. To make a long story short, I informed them they were going to give me the money that the church agree to give me and that if the church wants to do otherwise then they have that right. However, it would be the church's decision, not the Trustees' decision. We may have shared some excited words, but I left the meeting with my money and kept on Pastoring.

In retrospect, occasions like this one inspires my assertiveness about my compensation and insuring that Trustees remember that they don't have authority beyond what the church has agreed upon. It also inspires making clear the matters of my time off including vacation days, enrichment time, and allowing others to preach in my stead.

Two people in Bible study. I have always been faithful in teaching midweek Bible studies in addition to either teaching Sunday School, doing reviews of the lesson, or doing notes for the lesson. I remember that there were times at Mt. Moriah when the only people in Prayer Meeting and Bible Study were my wife and one other member. Yet I taught as if the sanctuary were filled.

Occasions like these help me appreciate having over 30 students in a Wednesday Bible study today. Thirty is less than I want, but it is a great deal more than I had. I can also see how such humble beginnings allowed me to work on my study and teaching skills that I used almost every week today.

Scratching my name off of the sign. My last Sunday at Mt. Moriah was my second and last Pastoral anniversary at this church. As expected, Zion packed the house out. People had to be turned away.

The members were kind to me in my Pastoral Anniversary offering, and the worship was edifying. I remember turning the keys into that one Deacon and leaving the church for the last time. The next morning, when I drove by the church, there was evidence that Sis. R. had taken her car keys and tried to scratch my name off of the church sign. There will be a special place for this person.

Occasions like this remind me that only what you do for Christ will last. It also reminds me that Sis. R. represented some but not even

1/4 of the people. Some times I can be guilty of thinking that the loudest mouth represents all of the silent people, when in reality, this can be far from the truth. If I had decided to stay, an overwhelming majority would have been glad for me to stay. For at least seven years after I left, members of Mt. Moriah would come to where I was preaching in the Buffalo area to support me. Nineteen years after I left, a number of the members from Mt. Moriah still came to my father's homegoing service to share their condolences with me. I walked; I didn't run to the exit of this ministry assignment.

Sis. Maggie Tyler and Sis. Kathy Washington. If nothing else happened at Mt. Moriah, the Lord allowed me to minister to and be ministered to by these two ladies. Sis. Tyler adopted my wife and I as essentially her children. She must have been 70+ years old. She helped renovate our house, donated generously towards my anniversary, and encouraged me to keep my head up. Sis. Washington joined the church as a result of my community evangelism and her standing outside the church window listening to me preach. I remember her inviting my family to her home to eat. I had the proud privilege of baptizing her, joining her in marriage to her husband (Ed), helping her get a job, and then seeing her join my father's church, after I left Mt. Moriah. She is my Facebook friend today - 23 years after I left.

My wife. During my Pastoralship at Mt. Moriah, my wife served as a staff secretary at Zion Missionary Baptist Church (i.e., where my father Pastored), but she also provided free clerical support for my ministry. She was very active with the young people of the church. And her greatest ministry was to help me stay encouraged, as I matriculated in the "University of Adversity."

Key Lessons From Mt. Moriah

From my time at Mt. Moriah, I learned the following key lessons:

1. Love but don't "be in love" with the church. I heard Senior Pastors talking about the Pastor being married to the church. With such a marriage in mind, I may have loved Mt. Moriah too much. In reality, I was not and no Pastor should be married to the church. Jesus and the church are husband and wife, not the Pastor and the church. At best, the Pastor is taking care of Jesus' bride

34

for Jesus. Thus, Pastors should love and respect the church as they would their father's or oldest brother's wife. But for Pastors to love the church as their own wife crosses a line. And it sets them up for terrible heartbreak.

2. Don't take it too personally. When you are the Pastor and people are mistreating you or not cooperating with you, you may think that the offense is against you. In reality, it is against the office. They were not mistreating you before or after you were the Pastor. And in some instances, they treated the Pastor before you and after you just about the same way they treated you.

3. Some churches want to remain small. On one hand, I had so much to learn about church growth and church health. But on the other hand, it was clear to me that everyone in the church did not want it to grow. That is why some actively discouraged people from joining or from staying. And those who did not actively discourage cooperated with the discouragement, by not doing their part. Don't assume that every small church wants to be a larger church.

4. The Bible is not authoritative truth for many of the members in the church. I remember two separate men talking about my convictions about the authority of scripture. One man, Bro. Lackey, commended me for being a Bible based Pastor. He said that one of my favorite phrases was "the Bible said." The second man, Dea. S., said that "when you say the Bible said, you think that everyone is supposed to simply do what you say." This latter mindset has been present in every church that I have Pastored.

On one hand, we are called to preach and teach the Bible, as if it is authoritative truth. And for the record, it is authoritative truth from God's perspective. But on the other hand, don't be surprised when even officers challenge, the authority of scripture. There is a challenge every time we fail to live up to God's word and essentially say "so what." But there is a deeper challenge when a person actually says, "that is what the Bible says, but this is the way we are going to do it." Guard your heart from being too disappointed by how spiritually immature officers in the church can be.

Chapter Three: Tucker Missionary Baptist Church

From my Pastoring Mt. Moriah, I now present my memories and reflections about Pastoring the Tucker Missionary Baptist Church, in Syracuse, New York. From 1991 to 1995, the Lord blessed this ministry. Over 260 membership candidates were received. The number of disciples (i.e., those who study, serve, and give) grew. A number of ministries were implemented such as the Men's Ministry, Community Evangelism Ministry, Training Union Ministry, and others. A Bible based constitution, budget/voucher system, and an enhanced fiscal accountability system were implemented. The church's revenue grew by 125%. A number of improvements were made to the facility, including the purchasing of several parcels of property. The church's reputation for Christian education, spirited worship, and community involvement were enhanced. The church had over $250,000 more assets, in 1995, than it had in 1990.

Memories and Reflections

Gospel Street Meetings. It was Pastor Bob Hope Robinson who showed me how to do a Gospel Street Meeting with a portable public address system, off the back of a pickup truck, and with free snack bags (i.e., cold cut sandwich, chips, apple, and juice) for those who came around. I added the ideas of collecting the names and contact information from those who gathered, so we could follow up on them after the session was over. We also gave them literature that talked about how to be saved and an invitation to come and join the church.

It was a joy to preach the gospel and have altar prayer for those in the community on a monthly basis. These experiences inspired my community evangelism work in Dayton, Ohio and beyond.

Radio. It was in Syracuse, New York that I started preaching on the radio on a regular basis. Because of the connections that one of my members had with the radio station, we were able to air about an hour of our worship service for about $100 a week.

This is where I learned that preaching during the time of other religious broadcasting may make you popular among church goers and religious people who listen to church services on the radio, but it doesn't really reach those who don't go to church. Our radio ministry may have been nice for our members who were shut in, but very few people joined the church because of it.

Correspondence degrees. I had completed my Bachelor's Degree in Community and Human Services, while in Buffalo, New York. In Syracuse, New York, I did not have the funds to go to an accredited seminary. The closest seminary that I was familiar with was about 75 miles away in Rochester, New York. My car was too unreliable, my money too short, and my focus too scattered to try to go to seminary, while in Syracuse, New York.

So I earned a Master's Degree in Pastoral Ministries (1994) and a Doctorate of Divinity Degree in Christian Family Studies (1995), from Christian Bible College and Seminary, in Independence, Missouri. Because of my personal efforts, I definitely learned valuable information from my studies. However, the requirements and the level of scrutiny from the school was very sparse.

Full time ministry. One great advantage of Tucker over Mt. Moriah for me was that it was a full time ministry position. Whereas I was working full time on non-church related jobs and Pastoring at Mt. Moriah, I was simply Pastoring Tucker.

This full time ministry allowed me to develop more thoughts regarding ministry. It was at Tucker that I coordinated my first youth retreat, first marriage retreat, and first church seminars. I remember having one of my role models, Dr. John Williams, come and do a teaching regarding discipleship development. He was so blessed and so generous that he gave me the honorarium that I gave him. I was not only blessed by the teaching and money, but I was also blessed by his example of generosity.

Tucker was also the place where I began teaching the Training Union material that I had developed while at Mt. Moriah. When the members that I Pastor today read these lines, they will probably chuckle. They kind of give me a hard time about my relentlessly requiring ministry managers, teachers, and follow-up workers to complete the Training Union material.

I also began to get somewhat involved in the denominational work, while at Tucker. I taught a class at both the Baptist association and state convention level. I attended association, state convention, and national convention level sessions.

Music staff. A surprising issue came about at Tucker regarding music staff. Up to this point, I had never heard of a director getting paid on an ongoing basis to direct the choir in addition to the musician. Mind you my wife was volunteering as the secretary because there was no office staff or volunteers.

To make a long story short, the director (i.e., a young man who joined under my Pastoralship) ended up getting paid with the church's agreement. But this occasion leads me to being very careful about people doing extra volunteer work, winning the hearts of the people, and then getting people to push for them being on the payroll. I try to make it very plain to volunteers that there is no money involved. I would rather that they be pleasantly surprised by an honorarium than for them to lobby for a salary.

A bad meeting. I remember having a bad church meeting in what I believe to be June of 1994. The essential issue was establishing that the Pastor was the chief executive officer, and the Trustees were to follow the Pastor's instructions in carrying out those things agreed to by the church.

What made the meeting bad was, first of all, the key Trustees were people appointed by me. These people had modest status in the church before my appointment, but yet they felt a need to challenge my authority and the clear teaching of the by-laws.

Second, a young lady whose name I will not mention came charging down the aisle as if she was going to attack me. Mind you we were in the sanctuary. Her father and others grabbed her, before she got to me. I don't remember if it was before or after these meeting that a Dea. H. called me a liar in a church meeting.

After seeing the young lady's disorder and my daughters in tears, I gathered my family (i.e., wife and two daughters) and went home. I left the meeting in the hands of an Associate Minister who was there. If I had to do it over again, I would have at least dismissed the meeting.

As I tried to calm myself down at my home, I heard some people on my porch. There were about 10 members who came to my home around 9:30 p.m. or 10 p.m. to apologize for what happen and to plead with me to stay with the church. In fact, the young lady's mother called me the next day to apologize for her daughter's behavior.

I was faithful in my service, until my last Sunday. However, within 90 days after that meeting, I had sent my resume to 100 known churches who were without a Pastor, and, within six months after the meeting, I was called to Pastor the Macedonia Missionary Baptist Church in Dayton, Ohio.

The members held an appreciation service for me. People shared tear filled testimonies about how my ministry had blessed them. The tension had decreased tremendously, but it was obvious that it was time for me to go. I am proud that I walked, I did not run to the exit of this ministry.

Bro. S. and Sis. Minnie Turner. I remember a young man who I will call Bro. S. He was suffering some mental illness that influenced his being rather disruptive to local worship services. I remember him being at a citywide worship service at a local church in Syracuse, New York and news cameras were rolling. He was walking around with a joint (i.e., marijuana cigarette) in his mouth and being generally disruptive, especially since no one was confronting him. The next Sunday, I told my church that I expected such behavior to be confronted and controlled with deliberate speed, if such was to happen at Tucker.

Well not too long after, Bro. S. came to Tucker. He watched me and I watched him, but he behaved himself. After maybe a few months, he joined the church. My wife was teaching the new members class. I was concerned with my wife being with him alone, but God was gracious. Today, I think I would have placed someone with my wife, if a person presented themselves as he did.

Bro. S. became a faithful member under my Pastoralship. In fact, he came to Buffalo, New York when I preached there, after I left Tucker. I believe he came to Dayton, Ohio to support one of my Pastoral Anniversaries. He taught me to be firm but fair in giving people a chance to prove themselves.

Sis. Minnie Turner was a blessed woman who lived in Florida during the winter and Syracuse doing the summer. She was a great blessing to my girls, by way of finances and wisdom. I remember she paid for my hotel room, when my wife and I went to Florida for a vacation and to preach at her other Pastor's church. My wife and daughters went on a separate occasion and spent time with her in Florida. Sis. Turner came to Macedonia in Dayton, Ohio on at least a couple of occasions. She has been to Buffalo, New York on a several occasions, when I was preaching in the area. And about once a year I hear from her even at the time of this writing (i.e., 19 years after leaving Syracuse, New York).

It should be noted that I have returned to Tucker on several occasions to preach for them. I have a high level of respect for Pastor

Leslie Johnson for consenting to this. He was the Pastor during my visits.

Key Lessons From Tucker

The following are key lessons that I acquired from my time at Tucker:

1. There is a difference between being a chaplain and being a Pastor. If I could have found peace with being a chaplain, I may have stayed at Tucker for much longer. To be a chaplain, as I am using the term, includes preaching and teaching that doesn't get too involved in what members should do for the church and how they should relate to the Pastor. There is a greater emphasis on how to be happy, have peace of mind, and endure the oppression that one experiences. Chaplaincy focuses on providing services like baptisms, weddings, funerals, hospital and home visitation, counseling, being a friendly greeter after worship, and representing the church at community and special personal functions like graduations. The chaplain focuses on services with almost no focus on equipping the saints for the work of the ministry.

If it is not obvious, I hold that the Pastor's job is to feed and lead the church. Feeding includes helping people understand their duty to the church and how to relate to the Pastor in addition to how to live the abundant life that God is calling us to live. Pastoring includes equipping the saints for the work of ministry, which includes modeling service but he/she should not be the hired servant of the church. As the leader, the Pastor is to lift the vision and manage the affairs related to making the vision a reality. This includes much more power than simply presiding over a meeting as an objective facilitator.

2. Don't be too afraid to leave. I am sure that there was some fear in my heart about leaving Tucker, even though I don't remember much. I am sure that I feared how it looked to be leaving my second church in only five years, at the age of 28, and with no accredited seminary training. I am sure that I had some fear about leaving the safety of being only 150 miles from my father and his resources. I am sure that I had some fears about was I jumping out of the frying pan into the fire. And of course, I had to consider the fact that I was carrying my wife and two young daughters with me.

But I thank God that God strengthened me for the move. I have a much more vivid memory of being excited than being afraid.

3. Get some things in writing. At the time of this writing, "Pastoral Contracts" are pretty common. However, in 1995, when I left Tucker to go to Macedonia, they were not as popular, especially for someone as young, inexperienced, and with so little accredited seminary. However, I was convinced from my previous experiences that such was necessary.

So before I said "yes" to going to my next church, we had some clear written agreements about compensation and authority. My recollection is that I came to Macedonia for $55,000, (i.e., about a $10k/yr. raise for me) out of about $150,000 a year of church's revenue. We agreed that my compensation would grow as the church's revenue would grow. We later explained this to mean that I would receive, as a bonus, 10% of the financial growth that took place under my administration. We agreed that the Pastor was the general manager of all church affairs, and his instructions are only vetoed by a majority church vote. We agreed that all officers were to be appointed by the Pastor, even though Deacons and Trustees also required the church's agreement. We agreed on an expense line and other items.

The point that I am making is to put stuff in writing, secure signatures, and make sure the documents are acknowledged in the minutes. Some of the things that you thought were understood may really not be understood. And some of the things that you all agreed to verbally will be forgotten, if not committed to writing. Seek wise counsel and good conscious about how much to put in writing before you go to the church, but don't be afraid of losing the church because you are trying to be clear about initial understandings and agreements regarding foundational issues (e.g., compensation and authority).

Chapter Four: Macedonia Missionary Baptist Church

From Pastoring Tucker, I now present my memories and reflections about Pastoring the Macedonia Missionary Baptist Church, in Dayton, Ohio. From 1994 to 2009, the Lord blessed this ministry in a mighty way. Over 930 membership candidates were received. The worship attendance grew from about 160 to about 225. The number of disciples (i.e., those who study, serve, and give) grew from 20 to over 150. Twenty ministry groups were added such as the Men's Ministry, Community Evangelism Ministry, Economic Empowerment Ministry, Crucial Link Ministry (i.e., ages 35 and 45 years old), Training Union Ministry, and others. A second worship service was added. A Bible based constitution, a budget/voucher system, and an improved fiscal accountability system were implemented. The church's revenue grew over 300% (i.e., from about $125,000 to over $400,000). Numerous facility improvements were made. Over $60,000 in scholarships were given and over $275,000 was given in local, home, and foreign missions.

A $1,100,000 multipurpose building was added to the church in 2007. This 9,000 square foot building was used for classes, programs, ministries, and gatherings. God blessed the church to develop a reputation for Christian education, relevant worship, youth programming, and community involvement.

Regarding community involvement, the church secured and paid for four houses, a commercial building, and several lots. The church financed year round youth development, economic empowerment, health, and community advocacy programming under its Macedonia Community Development Corporation (i.e., a separate 501(c)3 corporation). If the $600,000 mortgage was subtracted from the church's assets, it still had over $900,000 more assets, in 2009, than it had in 1993.

Memories and Reflections

Seminary. While Pastoring Macedonia, the Lord blessed me to be able to earn both my Master's of Divinity Degree and my Doctorate of Ministry Degree from the United Theological Seminary. I graduated when the campus was in Dayton, Ohio. Since my graduations, the campus has moved to a suburb of Dayton - Trotwood, Ohio.

Every since I started preaching, I have had a strong desire to be academically prepared for ministry. I did well in elementary school, high school, and college. Even before I did correspondence degrees in Syracuse, New York, I read on a regular basis. My father and some of the senior Pastors in Dayton encouraged me to focus on getting my seminary education, before or instead of getting too busy with denominational or community affairs.

As I recall, I started my Master's Degree with no transfer credits for experience or academic equivalence, in 1996. Taking two or three classes when I could and every now and then four classes, I completed my 90 credit hour Master's of Divinity Degree in 2000. My focus was New Testament Urban Churches.

To say that it was challenging to keep my grades up (i.e., the equivalent of an A or B), while Pastoring full time, and being an active family man would be an understatement. But by the grace of God, I did it. I used my Pastoral expense line from my church and student loans to finance my education. I had no scholarships or grants. After I completed my degree, I used my Pastoral expense line to pay off the student loans.

I started my Doctorate of Ministry Degree in 2001 and finished in 2003. My focus was on economic and spiritual empowerment in Black churches. Surprisingly, the academic rigor of the Master's was more intense than that of my Doctorates. However, I had to do more original thinking and composing of my thoughts, which was not a big problem for my personality type. In other words, expressing my opinion and explaining/arguing my rational comes rather naturally for me (smile).

From my seminary experiences, I learned that so much can be accomplished with the proper management of time and energy. I remember studying in as small as 15 minute blocks of times, getting up at 6 a.m., and working until 9:30 - 10:00 p.m., Monday through at least Thursday with about 4-6 hours of study on Friday and Saturday.

I was amazed at how God could show me how what I was studying in school, Sunday School, Wednesday Bible Study, and sermon preparation often complimented one another. Seminary taught me to raise different questions and to be less dogmatic about so many things, even though I have my preferences and sometimes convictions.

I thank God for my seminary education and the timing. If I had went earlier, I would have assumed that all "White" was right (i.e., European opinions treated as absolute truths). If I had went much later, I would have been to set in my ways to learn anything new. My Pastoral experience helped me filter out some of the unhelpful theories and culturally unhelpful material, while focusing on those things that would be beneficial in my practice of ministry.

I am convinced as never before that we know in part and therefore we preach in part. I am not afraid to say that I don't know. In fact, I have learned that some people don't know that they don't know. They are so fixated on their opinion that they are not aware of how much faith is being used in holding to their opinion. A quick example may be the use of the King James Version of the Bible. There are still those who believe that the one and only version of the Bible is the King James Version of the Bible.

Seminary helped me see that Whites, Blacks, and Asians are all walking by faith. No group is naturally smarter or more academically challenged. And we all have challenges with Pastoring in our contexts.

Women Clergy. Besides changing from the King James Version to the New International Version of the Bible, as my primary preaching and teaching translation, one of the most controversial changes in my ministry has been the acceptance of female clergy. I self-published a book, *Our Preaching Sisters*, in 2000. I taught a class to my church on how my convictions had changed from being anti-female clergy to being pro-female clergy.

First, my church was surprisingly accepting. The great majority of the members were willing to accept whatever the Pastor wanted in this area. Of course, there were some who were opposed. In fact, a few members left the church. During my stay at Macedonia, I had one woman who earned her ministry license under my administration and a handful of women to preach.

Second, some of my colleagues abandoned me, since I had drifted from the popular conservative anti-female clergy understanding. In fact, I was put out of the Baptist Minister's Union in Dayton, Ohio, because I believed in female clergy. I didn't even have a female preacher at that time and never sought to bring them to the Union, but because I believed in them, I was not welcomed.

One of my preaching role models broke the fellowship between our churches over this issue. This was so irrational to me. It was made even more irrational by the fact that those who did not want to fellowship with me in Dayton, Ohio fellowshipped with me and other Pastors who had female clergy in our state convention and national convention. I was a state officer and taught classes at both the association and state levels. In other words, I was teaching at the association and state those I could not preach to in Dayton, all because of women clergy.

From this experience, I learned that God is so faithful. Had I not been ostracized by my conservative Baptist brothers, I would not have been elected to serve as the Co-President of Leaders for Equality and Action in Dayton, President of the Dayton unit of the National Association for Colored People, and probably not have had the energy to start the Macedonia Community Development Corporation. Had I not been ostracized by my conservative Baptist brothers, I may have never had the preaching opportunities among Methodist and others that I enjoyed. And I would have thought that brothers would never do such a thing to especially me.

Community Involvement. Remember that my undergraduate degree is in Community and Human Services. So I have had a long-term passion for helping to improve the quality of life for both communities and individuals. I had marvelous opportunities to work in the community, as I Pastored Macedonia.

From 2000 – 2004, I served as the Co-President for Leaders for Equality and Action in Dayton (i.e., L.E.A.D.). This organization, which was composed of over ten churches and faith communities (i.e., combined membership of over 8,000 members) focused on local justice issues. I am proud of the following accomplishments:

- We hired a full time organizer.

- We persuaded the city to expand its living wage ordinance.

- We persuaded the Police Chief to implement LEAD's "Hot Spot Cards" and give extra effort to community policing.

- We persuaded the school superintendent to take a serious look at Direct Instruction.

It was good to work with Whites and Blacks, Christians and non-Christians, and several denominations of Christians (e.g., Baptist, Methodist, Presbyterian, and Episcopalian as I recall). It was good to see the training and structure used to build a community organizing organization.

There were too many meetings and too much reliance of the Robert's Rules of Order for me. However, I feel good about my performance of my duties.

From 2004 to 2006, I served as the President of the Dayton unit of the National Association for the Advancement of Colored People. I am proud of the following accomplishments:

- The unit became one of the fifty largest branches in the country.

- Our Youth Council was recognized as the number one Council in the nation.

- Our unit fought off state budget cuts.

- We were one of the leading groups that raised over $27,000 for Hurricane Katrina relief and worked collaboratively to send over twenty truckloads of items to the Gulf Coast area, in 2005.

- We played a key role in fighting off the discriminatory efforts to cut minority health services in the Dayton, Ohio area.

- I left the unit $20,000 stronger than when I came to office, received a leadership award for my service, and was supportive of the new President, who served faithfully, as my Vice President.

However, I learned that I am not a good politician. I am at my best just getting my work done, in budget and on time with my team. I am at my worse, when I have to pretend and socialize with people I don't trust. The latter situation is so draining to me. I remember having to bite my tongue because my unit needed funds and cooperation from the people I was talking to. I had to remember that I was wearing my dependent President's hat, instead of my independent Pastor's hat.

From 1997 to 2009, I founded and served as the President of the Macedonia Community Development Corporation. This corporation was the transformation of volunteer efforts and ideas into a 501(c)3 certified non-profit corporation with a mission of improving the quality of life on the west side of Dayton, Ohio and vicinity. I am proud of the following accomplishments:

- We formed a respected board of trustees, received corporate funds, and seven programs were implemented.

- The Junior and Young Villagers Programs focused on weekly life enrichment teaching, mentoring, as well as year round community service, recreation, and enrichment projects.

- The Academic Enrichment Program focused on tutoring, parent/caregiver involvement, and managing the $4,000+/year scholarship funds.

- The Economic Empowerment Program focused on financial literacy, support groups, and urging communal economic empowerment through patronage, a faith-based credit union, and housing.

- The Housing Program featured the leasing of four houses and a commercial building, in addition to the purchase, renovation, and selling of a 24 unit apartment complex, which used to be an eye sore and den of drugs and violence.

- The Health Program focused on weekly "Healthy Living Classes" (i.e., exercising and health tidbits), year round health focuses, blood and organ donations, and health fairs promotion.

- The Community Advocacy Program successfully facilitated the creation of a block club, provided supportive services to the

NAACP and Urban League, and successfully lobbied for issues like blocking liquor saturation, expanding the living wage ordinance in the city, and preventing the cutting of the local government fund at the state level. Voter registration and education was a staple of the program.

- As the President of Macedonia Community Development Corporation, I was elected to be a founding co-convener (i.e., co-president) of the Dayton Community Revitalization Network (i.e., a network of about 10 community based organizations focused on improving the quality of life on the west side of Dayton through collaborative efforts).

I wish I had spent more time developing my funding research and grant proposal writing skills. If I had to do it again, I would give extra thought to naming the community development corporation after the church that I Pastored. The name may have discouraged some others from being involved at a higher level.

In addition to the three larger assignments above, I cannot remember all of the committees and ad hoc projects that I worked on. I am proud to say that our church gave over $275,000 to local efforts during my watch. The church had earned a reputation for being very involved in the community. It was not strange for the mayor, school superintendent, city commissioners, school board members, and others to visit the church and to seek my advice on various issues.

Denominational Involvement. Macedonia allowed me to do some good work in the Baptist denomination.

From 2004 to 2009, I served as the elected President of the Northwestern Baptist District Association's Congress, after having served as the General Secretary, Vice Moderator, and one of the instructors. I am proud of the following accomplishments:

- We implemented a scholarship program, which awarded over $2,000.

- We developed curriculum, in response to survey and interviews with Pastors.

- We led the Congress into its first profitable year, in known history.

- We recruited young, middle aged, and senior Pastors into the teaching ministries, in record numbers.

From 2000 to 2004, as the Second Vice Moderator, I am proud of the following accomplishments:

- We implemented a scholarship program and awarded over $1,000.

- We implemented a greater level of productivity and organization to our business meetings, in part because of my being allowed to preside over many of the meetings.

I also served as an elected Secretary, taught several courses, and preached on a number of occasions throughout the district.

From 2000 to 2009, I taught a couple of courses at the Ohio Baptist General Convention's Congress of Christian Education (e.g., evangelism and stewardship). I served as a Vice President of the Congress, Parliamentarian for the parent body, Chairman of the Young Pastor's Project, and worked with the Street Evangelism Ministry. I preached in both the convention and at a number of convention churches during my Pastorate at Macedonia.

From my denominational work, I have grown convinced that the only way to get something done is to have a team of Pastors who are committed to supporting a vision with their influence and finances. If you win the popular vote, but don't have Pastoral support, you will not get very far in denominational work. Gaining Pastoral support requires a significant amount of time and energy being given to one-on-one conversations, small groups, and trust building.

Deacon (Dea.) Ed Love. Before I close my thoughts about Macedonia, I have to make mention of Dea. Ed Love. Dea. Love was already a Deacon by the time I came to Macedonia. He proved to be a great asset to my ministry and the church. Those who don't know the whole story would think that I am appreciative of Dea. Love because he was my "yes man" - said "yes" to whatever I said with no critical reflection of feedback. But Dea. Love and I know the truth is that we differed on a number of items. I remember a disagreement about my compensation and about putting a gym in the multipurpose space. The fact is that when there was a strong difference of opinion, I may have been more inclined to say "yes" to him than to push forward with my idea.

Dea. Love was a model of informed followership. He would speak his mind with respect and humility and then followed leadership trusting that God would see that things worked out. What more could you ask?

I believe that his encouragement and support helped me stay at Macedonia for as long as I did. I know that he made my stay more enjoyable than it would have been otherwise. We still talk about twice a year. But we respect our boundaries and positions enough to avoid detailed conversations about either church. I wish there were a way for him to come and join Southern Baptist Church. God bless Dea. Ed Love and his family.

My family. While I was Pastoring, going to school, and working in both the community and denomination, my wife was working very hard as well. She earned her Bachelor's

Degree from Wilberforce University in 2000. Her focus was on organizational management. She earned her Master's Degree from Wright State University in 2004. Her focus was on African American families. I am so proud of her tenacity. She is the first one in her family to complete a college degree. She made so many sacrifices to support my ministry goals.

She worked as my ministry assistant at Macedonia, as an officially part time staff person, even though she often worked full time hours. She worked tirelessly to manage our apartments. I thank God that the church allowed us to use church funds to help pay for her degrees.

As for our girls, both of them did well in school. They earned scholarships to go to college. And they were doing well in college and living in their own apartments, before my wife and I left the area.

Time to move on. When you have been at a church for over 10 years, you cannot blame much on your predecessor. After about 12 years, I was talking to my senior officers about how the church is not growing like I thought that it would and how I was disturbed by how we missed our five year goals for newer members, attendance, and ministry development. I remember one of the ladies who was in her 40's at the time saying that she did not want the church to get too big (i.e., 500 or more), while we were seeing only 225 people on Sunday at that time. It was not just her. There were others who were perfectly comfortable with the lack of or limited church growth.

I was conflicted. Personally, I was doing well. I had a six-figure compensation package, paid for home, and no student loans on my Doctorate Degree nor my wife's Master's Degree. There were those suggesting that I should run for various denominational offices, others suggesting that I run for political office, and there was the allure of developing the community development corporation into a greater staff position. However, I was also convicted that as it related to Pastoring, I would be coasting. And coasting from my early 40's to 65 years old or more was too much coasting.

So I put out some resumes. As I recall, well over half of the resumes that I sent out called me. I talked with representatives on the phone, and we agreed that there was no need to talk any further, in light of my compensation requirements. The only church that seemed worth pursuing was the one that I eventually went to. I was just about ready to get comfortable in Dayton, knowing that I had given effort to going to a larger assignment.

It really did my heart good to be able to give the church a 90 day notice. Our separation was so peaceful that Macedonia came to my installation in Cincinnati, in 2009. And Southern came to Macedonia's Church Anniversary, in 2013. I walked; I didn't run to the exit.

From this I learned that God has a plan. The plan is not always about what is best for you as an individual. It is often about what is good for the whole and in the long run.

Key Lessons From Macedonia

1. Walk, don't run to the exit. I am so thankful for the relationship that I still enjoy with Macedonia. At least 75 of them came to my installation at Southern Baptist Church. I have preached there on two occasions and have shared great fellowship with Dr. Hunter, my successor. My oldest daughter stayed there, after my wife and I left. She served on the staff for a period and was licensed to preach.

I believe this is evidence that I left the right way. There are some Pastors who are not welcomed at their previous churches. I urge every Pastor to walk, don't run to the exit of a church. In other words, be very prayerful and give adequate time for transition. I gave Macedonia 90 days; however, I think that is some cases, 30 days would be fine.

2. Don't be too comfortable to leave. I was comfortable in Dayton. I had a six figure income, a paid for house, no fights at my church, and great respect in my community. But because I believed that it was God's will to move on, I moved on.

I believe that because my heart was right, God has shown great favor on my ministry at Southern. I would urge my readers to always listen to and obey God's will, instead of simply staying in what appears to be a comfortable situation. God can make things uncomfortable, if we stop obeying His will.

71

3. Friendships. As I look back over my Pastoral career, I have shared some significant friendships. I feel good about my efforts to develop friendships, even though I don't have a great deal of fruit to show for my work.

On one hand, I suspect that my goal and task orientation accompanied by impatience can be a little bit of a turn off. I can be a little intense with my passion for knowledge, wealth accumulation, and progress.

But on the other hand, I would rather have few true friends than to waste my time with fake friends. I would rather have a few true friends who accept me as I am, instead of those who are trying to change me. I would urge my readers to give serious effort to friendship development with the realization that if you find two or three close friends, you have found pure gold.

Chapter Five: Southern Baptist Church

From Pastoring Macedonia, in this chapter, I present my memories, reflections, and dreams related to Pastoring the Southern Baptist Church, in Cincinnati, Ohio. From 2009 to present, the Lord has blessed this ministry. Over 480 membership candidates were received. The number of disciples (i.e., those who study, serve, and give) has grown from about 125 to over 215. Eight ministry groups were implemented including the Men Ministry, Economic Empowerment Ministry, Community Evangelism Ministry, Community Involvement Ministry, Training Union Ministry, and others. A second weekly Bible Study was added. The church was led into volunteering over 1,700 accountable hours a year and giving over $11,000 a year in local, home, and foreign missions. The by-laws were updated and aligned with the Word of God. Leadership transparency and financial accountability were enhanced. *One million dollars worth of debt was paid off.* Physical improvements were made (e.g., roofs, bathrooms, kitchen, etc.). Even though attendance has dropped from about 350 to about 325 and the real revenue has dropped from about $945,000 to about $880,000, the church is still stronger in discipleship, ministries, and community involvement as well as over $1,000,000 better off today than it was in 2008.

Memories and Reflections

The call. As I recall, I had preached for Pas. Oliver Williams, in Cincinnati, Ohio. He told me about Southern being without a Pastor. I sent a resume. It took about a year for the process to play out. I preached a couple of times, taught a class, met with a number of people, interviewed, and submitted to credit checks, criminal checks, and drug testing.

As I understand it, the vote was rather close because the beloved Interim Pastor became a candidate. Even though I offered him a staff position, he resigned and started another church. Less than 25 members went with him from Southern.

It would not be proper to disclose financial figures, but allow me to say that it was a financial promotion from what I was getting paid in Dayton, Ohio. In fact, I hired my wife, with the church's blessings, in my first year, as a part time staff person. This made the move an even greater financial promotion.

Disappointments.   At this point, I want to tell my story, without being unnecessarily offensive to those who have caused some of my grief. The following are my greatest disappointments in coming to Southern:

- I was led to believe that Southern collected $1.1 million a year in revenue and that the houses and childcare center were making money for the church. In reality, we collected more like $945,000 and both the houses and childcare center were costing the church thousands of dollars a year (i.e., at least $10,000 a year with mortgage free houses and at least $25,000 a year with the childcare's health insurances).

- I was given rather vague information about attendance. The attendance numbers ranged from a couple of thousand to 500. In reality, 350 would have been a more accurate number.

- I was given misleading information about Southern being a pillar of the community. In reality, Pas. Milton was rather active in the community. His greatest claim to fame may be his involvement in the establishment of the town center (i.e., a shopping plaza a short walk across the street from the church with about 20 retail stores that employs about 100 people). There are no records of the church's money being involved, nor the church receiving any money from the project. However, the church had little verifiable involvement in the community. In fact, some of those in the neighborhood talk about the members being snobbish towards the poor and working class.

- I overestimated the level of discipleship and leadership maturity that I was starting with. I thought that there would be more people who loved God enough to serve as ministry managers, teachers, follow-up workers, and general workers. It is becoming more and more difficult to find people to keep the ministries operating at a high level.

- And then I remember early power struggles among selected trustees and a deacon or two. One of the most troubling trustees is dead, several left or became rather inactive, and the most troubling deacon was placed on inactive status as of January 2015. Behind the scenes, I have dealt with trustees wanting me to sign in or punch a time clock. I have been asked to remit a $30 meal expense on my credit card, while a former staff person misappropriated at least $16,000. I have wasted energy talking about how the Bible is more important than a deacon's emotions and the opinions of his mysterious group of members.

In spite of all of my disappointments, ***the good has far outweighed the bad at Southern***. I have no regrets about coming to Southern. It just would have been nice to have a clearer picture of what I was getting into and who I had to work with.

From my disappointments, I have learned that no matter how careful you are in trying to discern if a move is right for you or not, there is an element of faith. If you trust God, God will work things out for the good of His people. Do your best with faith in God, and trust God with the rest.

Accomplishments. God has been so faithful. The following are my proudest accomplishments over the last six years:

- Over 480 people have responded to the invitation to join or rejoin the church.

- Many of those who did not want to be under my administration are gone and yet there remains an average attendance of 325. We see about 105 at 7:30 a.m. And we see about 220 in our 10:45 a.m. worship service.

- We have 215 disciples compared to about 125 in 2008 and 62 active Training Union graduates. Disciples, as used here, are those who we have records of their studying, serving, and giving at least $10/week. An active Training Union graduate is one who has completed the following courses, which are two to four hours of class time and some homework: Membership Orientation, Discipleship Orientation, Leadership Orientation, Bible and Doctrine Overview, Church and Her Mission, and then one of the following workshops: Management, Teaching, or Follow-Up, including about three months of fieldwork.

- We have 29 need meeting ministries. I thank God for His allowing us to add or significantly revamp the following ministries: Membership Orientation, Discipleship Development, Training Union, Wednesday Bible Study (i.e., added a noon Bible Study), Men, Women, Economic

Empowerment, Senior, Community Evangelism, Follow-up Evangelism, Each Reach One, and Community Involvement Ministries as well as children and youth ministry on Wednesday (i.e., Boys to Men I and II).

- We are an active partner in improving the quality of life in Avondale and vicinity. By the grace of God, in 2014, we can account for approximately 2,000 volunteer hours and over $14,000 worth of donations to organizations beyond our church. All ministry groups are strongly requested and held accountable for volunteering at one or more of the following organizations: National Association for the Advancement of Colored People, Drop Inn Center, Every Child Succeed, Avondale Community Council, Urban League, and more. We donate to organizations and causes like Historically Black Colleges and Universities, foreign mission work in Africa, Haiti, and India as well as various disasters that come up from time to time.

- We have made some structural improvements. It gives me great joy to know that our by-laws have been revamped and built on biblical principles. If something happened to me today, the church has written and agreed upon guidelines for how to call another Pastor. The financial transparency has been greatly increased. There is an income and expense financial statement disbursed every quarter to the congregation that shows in a rather itemized fashion how we are doing in relationship to our agreed upon budget. We have a system to update our membership roster annually to insure all members are cared for and those who are not being active are not draining the church's resources or causing trouble. Having finished our 2014 strategic plan, we are starting our strategic plan for 2020.

- Under physical improvements, we have done significant roof and ceiling work, remodeled the kitchen, completely rehabbed two bathroom areas, and replaced some of the most worn out awnings that you have ever seen (smile). I estimate that we have spent at least $80,000 on significant physical improvements and repairs, in addition to normal repair and maintenance expenses of at least $80,000 a year. In spite of all of that, we still paid off $1,000,000 of debt that I inherited. This will free up $200,000 a year to allow for renovations, a little extra staff, and some breathing room. Praise the Lord!

Pastor Eugene Ellington and Reverend Ed Lige. I am still very thankful for two special people. Pastor Eugene Ellington and Reverend Ed Lige traveled at their expense and without my prior knowledge from Cincinnati, Ohio to Buffalo, New York to be by my side, as I performed the eulogy at my father's homegoing service, in September 2011. They were both by my side again, when I performed the eulogy for my mother in-law, in February 2013.

I wrote about my dealing with my father's death in my book entitled, ***From Skippers, Virginia to Eternal Life: A Salute to Rev. Dr. Robert E. Baines, Sr. and Lessons for Those Yet on the Journey*** (Amazon.com, 2012).

From these accomplishments and "special thanks," I have learned that God can do great things, in spite of how things look to us. In spite of new members not staying, members leaving, and finances dropping, all of the above and more were accomplished. Only God can take credit for what has been accomplished.

My Family. My wife is doing a great job of life coaching, doing personal fitness training, and teaching healthy living courses outside the church and serving on my staff at Southern. As a staff person, she works with newer members, Sunday School, Wednesday Bible Study, Discipleship Development, and Training Union Ministries as well as the Men, Women, Marriage Enrichment, Singles, and Senior Ministries. I am very thankful for her people skills.

Both of our daughters are college graduates and Gospel Ministers. Our oldest daughter has a Master's Degree in Public Administration and works for Montgomery County (i.e., in Ohio) as essentially a social worker on her way to being a part of management. She stayed at Macedonia, where she announced her call to preach and was licensed, after I left.

Our youngest daughter has a Bachelor's degree in Organizational Leadership and a cosmetology license. She went to Mt. Pisgah Missionary Baptist Church, in Dayton, Ohio, after I left. There she was licensed to preach, after she announced her call to preach under my ministry at Macedonia. She and her husband (Min. Jared Davis) just blessed us with our first grandchild - Jared Aston Davis, Jr. (JJ).

My Dreams for Southern Baptist Church

I pray that the following dreams are from the Lord and not simply my own ambitions. To be honest, they may be a mixture of both. I dream of seeing at least the following, by the time I reach age 65 and at least semi-retired (i.e., 17 years from now):

- A total of 1,200 people would have come to join or rejoin the church during my time at Southern.

- Average attendance of 150 at 7:30 a.m. and 350 at 10:45 a.m. worship.

- We will have 300 registered disciples and 75 active Training Union graduates to manage our 40 need meeting ministries. Among the need meeting ministries will be Men, Women, Singles, Marriage Enrichment, and Seniors Ministries. Each of these ministry groups will have at least quarterly enrichment teachings, service projects, and fellowship activities along with accountability partnerships to support the discipleship development of those involved. The ministries would include an Economic Empowerment Ministry that helps members with gainful employment, business development, financial literacy and support, home ownership, and more. The ministries would include a Health Ministry that helps members with healthy living education and support, especially around issues like diet, exercise, stress management, cancer, diabetes, and hypertension. The ministries will include vibrant children, youth, and young adult ministries that help young people develop the skills, knowledge, and character to live an abundant life that glorifies God. Tutoring, scholarships, financial aid assistance, and mentoring will be in place. Every faithful young person will receive at least $1,000 from their church family after high school and at least $200 a year while in college.

- We will be known for volunteering 5,000 hours a year (i.e., 10 x 500 average Sunday attendance) to improving Avondale and vicinity as well as donating $110,000 a year (i.e., 10% of our $1.1 million revenue). We will strategically place our members on boards and committees to insure that we are playing a vital role in the improvement of our community and helping people with their personal and financial development, while advocating for justice and equitable disbursement of resources.

- We will have no debt, a nice looking and very functional building, and a $1,000,000 endowment. The endowment will allow us to give an extra $50,000 a year in donations and scholarships. We will have adequate staff, including a very capable assistant or co-Pastor. At this time, I find myself wresting with the call to equip the saints for the work of the ministry (see Eph. 4:11-13) and the temptation to outsource a larger portion of the work of the ministry to staff. I would guess that we will end up with a mixture of staff and unpaid volunteers.

My Personal Vision and Legacy

I want to live so that people can truly say the following:

Dr. Baines lived as if his core values were to love God and others, as he loved himself. They would probably say that I loved God, loved people, and took good care of myself. They would say that I was proud of my African American/Black heritage.

Dr. Baines was spiritually mature, took care of his health and finances, worked on his personal development, learned to be pleasant and need responsive, and learned to enjoy the journey of his life.

Dr. Baines demonstrated deep love for his wife, children, grandchild, mother, and sister. He gave more than he took from close friendships, was available for friendships, and loved his extended family.

Dr. Baines was a great asset to his community and denomination. They will be able to point to at least 40 awards and certificates of appreciation for ministry and work in the Cincinnati area. They will be able to point to my charitable giving and volunteer service focused on Avondale uplift, Black economic empowerment, young people development, breast and prostate cancer research, and disaster relief. They will be able to point to the Dr. Robert E. Baines, Jr. Scholarships, the Daphene Baines Scholarships, a list of 25 people whom I have significantly influenced to make a noted impact for Christ, 50

Christian living books (see RobertBaines.org) and a $100,000 legacy fund to insure that my giving of $12,000 a year will continue long after my demise.

Chapter Six: Let the Church Say "Amen"

From my thoughts about Pastoring Southern Baptist Church, I now focus on lessons I want to be remembered for. It is rather common for the Black Pastor to urge the congregation to say "amen," as a way of the church showing affirmation and agreement with what is being said. The following are 9 things I want every reader to remember about me. At the core of my preaching, teaching, and ministry are these lessons for living:

1. I am a grace case. On one hand, I am richly blessed. At the age of 48, I am saved, physically fit, celebrating 30 years of being happily married, both of my daughters are college graduates and Gospel Ministers, and I have a grand son. I have no financial worries.

I have had the highest degree in my field for 11 years. My wife has a Master's Degree and serves on my church staff. Even at an average Sunday attendance of 325, Southern exceeds more than about 90% of the churches in America. Our church is debt free.

I feel good about my work in the church and community.

But on the other hand, I know that I don't deserve any of the above. In my heart, I really wish that I were a stronger disciple of Christ. This is not the venue to air dirty laundry. Let me simply say that if it had not been for the grace of God, I would not be anywhere near where I am. When someone says that I am arrogant or I think of myself more highly than I ought, I believe that they are confusing my confidence in God's anointing of my sinful life with what appears to be arrogance. My having received so much grace helps me to keep working on being gracious towards others.

2. Be a disciple of Christ. By this I mean make sure that you are saved and striving to live according to God's word. Make sure that you have accepted Jesus as your savior by faith (see Jn. 3:16). No one lives well enough to be right with God. Salvation comes only through the substitutionary death payment of Jesus, by faith.

Live by God's word, which calls for your knowing God's word. Develop the habit of having quiet time. Make at least 10 minutes a day to read a passage of scripture, make some bullet notes about how to live by it, and pray for God's wisdom, courage, and energy to live by the passage. If you are not an active member of a Bible preaching and teaching church and if you are not one who studies, serves, and gives then you have a significant amount of work to do with your discipleship.

There are principles in God's word for every area of our lives. Find and live by God's principles. The philosophies of this world and our own sense of right and wrong are totally unreliable. Jesus is the light of the world. You will experience your greatest satisfaction and fulfillment, as you discover and obey God's will for your life. You will always be dissatisfied and unfulfilled unto you surrender to God's will for your life. There is a hole that cannot be filled, a thirst that cannot be quenched, and a hunger that cannot be satisfied, until you are right and tight with God - saved and working on your discipleship.

3. Take care of your health. It is clear to me that having money, relationships, and accomplishments without your health leaves you lacking. I exercise five days a week - walk/jog for one hour a day on Monday, Wednesday, and Friday; 100 push-ups, abdominal work, and stretching on Tuesday and Thursday. I normally drink three liters of water a day, load up on fruits and vegetables, eat poultry and nuts, and strive to minimize my eating of sweets and processed food. I routinely get seven to eight hours of sleep. I get a physical every year, go to the dentist, and get my eyes checked. Take care of your health.

4. Be a wise steward of your finances. On one hand, there are those who struggle to pay for the basics of life - food, clothing, and shelter. I say to this group do your best to become gainfully employed or run your own profitable business. Do whatever it takes to earn an honest living. College is not for everyone, especially with the growing cost of tuition. But trade school or something should be pursued, if at all possible.

On the other hand, there are those who are able to pay for the basics of life and at least a little more. To this group, I say strive to live the 10/10/80 principle. Give God at least 10% of your gross income (i.e., tithes). Save and invest at least 10%. Develop a three to nine month emergency fund. Invest in retirement accounts as soon as possible, even if you only have $10 a week to invest. Live on 80% or less of your income. For many this will mean cutting coupons, eating generic foods, and wearing no named or used clothes. It may mean buying three to five year old cars and driving to affordable vacation spots, instead of flying.

Home ownership, living debt free, and passing wealth on to responsible people should be a part of your spiritual agenda. There is nothing holy about being poor. In too many cases, poverty in America is a product of both sinful systems and poor individual stewardship. Retirement is for those with money, not just those who get old. Take care of your finances, so you will not be 80 years old working at McDonalds or Walmart.

5. Invest in family and friends. I thank God for my wife and children. I am thankful for my mother and sister. At each church that I have Pastored, the Lord has blessed me with special relationships among the church members and in the communities.

I believe that to a great extent, we reap what we sow. If we sow into relationships, we can reap from them. I have found this to be especially true of my marriage and with my children.

However, there is also a such thing as sowing good seed into bad ground. There are those who don't seek friendship that is mutually beneficial. Some are simply consumers. They take all that you give and yet seek for more. Some are constant complainers and will some how spoil the brightest day. Some are jealous or intimidated by you and what God has done in your life. Dr. Maya Angelou is given credit for saying something like "when people show you who they are, believe them, the first time." Don't keep sowing good seeds into bad ground.

On the other hand, don't stereotype all ground as bad because of your previous experiences. Appreciate that some people are specialty friends. That is, they are good for going to football games but not the best person to talk to about politics. Some are great for talking about politics but not family matters.

Life can be sweeter when experienced in relationships where there is mutual enjoyment, trust, and cooperation. These relationships should be sought after and nurtured.

6. Make a contribution. Rev. Al Sharpton is given credit for saying something like there is nothing more troubling than for a Pastor to have to give a eulogy for someone and the deceased has done nothing relevant. A philosopher, William James, is given credit for saying something like the value of life is found in its donation, not duration.

In each of these ideas is what I am calling "contribution." Do something to help somebody else. Touch someone along your life's journey. If I talked about my ministry, website, books, and donations, you may excuse yourself, by saying that you don't have it like I have it.

So let me make mention of my deceased mother-in-law, Sis. Beatrice Tucker. She did not graduate from high school, never made $20,000 a year, and raised her four children primarily by herself. But yet she touched people everywhere she went. She made time to love on children, watch after seniors (even when she was a senior), and say hello with a smile to everyone she met.

Instead of focusing on what you cannot do, focus on what you can do. Help somebody along your life's journey. Live so that someone feels duty bound to come to your homegoing (i.e., funeral) service to show their respects. Give some child a card with a few dollars in it because of a good report card or because of their showing good manners. Call the homebound members in the bulletin. Help a family during the holiday season. Make a contribution.

7. Get focused. In Stephen Covey's book, ***The Seven Habits of Highly Effective People***, he talks about imagining what you want people to say about you at your funeral. What do you want family members, friends, co-workers, and community people to say about you? Next, live in such a way that they would have reason to say what you want them to say. In other words, live the way you want to be remembered, because we are going to remember how you lived. And more importantly, God is going to hold you accountable for how you have lived.

Focus is a natural strength of mine. But if it were not then I would have to work on it like I work on being more patient, which is not a natural strength of mine. Through prayer, soul searching, and wise counsel, seek to understand the goals that God wants you to pursue for this year, the next five years, and your life. Plan your work, work your plan, and make adjustments as needed. You would be surprised by how much you will accomplish, if you get focused and work every day on your goals for the next three years. On the other hand, you can easily be like so many people who will live for the next three years and not only have very little to show for it, but they had no plans for what they were even trying to do.

8. Enjoy the journey. After 25 years of Pastoring, I am convinced, as never before, that we don't know what is going to happen in our lives. Today, we can have all kinds of plans for the next five years with the benefits of good health, supportive relationships, and a strong financial footing. But in the morning, we can be sick from disease or crippled by injury. Relationships and finances can fade in unexpected ways and at the most inopportune times.

No matter how busy you are, how broke you are, and how sick or tired you are, make time to focus on something enjoyable everyday. One of my recently developed habits is to announce at least three things that I am thankful for in the morning (i.e., while walking/jogging or during breakfast), at 2:00 p.m., and at 9:00 p.m. I have daily alarms set to remind me to stop and give thanks for at least three things three times a day.

It is easy to forget what a blessing it is to have food to eat, clean clothes to wear, and a shelter over our heads. It is easy to forget how blessed we are to be able to walk, use the bathroom by ourselves, and read a book. There are those who would pay good money to be in church one more time, to be free from prison walls, or to be able to take a deep breath of fresh air without coughing.

9. Make death preparations. No matter how well we take care of our health and live for Jesus, death is on the way. Instead of living in denial or trying to ignore this reality, get your house in order. It may border on being irresponsible for you to be especially the head of a household and don't have some basic things in order. Make sure you have some burial insurance. Ten thousand dollars will pay for a traditional funeral and leave your loved ones a little change.

My wife and I are registered with Wright State University as body donors. When we die, our bodies are to be picked up or taken to Wright State University, where they will use our bodies to train medical students and perform medical research. We will then be cremated and our ashes put in a mass area with others. For us, this is a charitable act that we pray leads to medical advances. We believe to be absent from the body is to be present with the Lord (see II Cor. 5:8). We would prefer people to look at pictures of how we lived, instead of our corpse or casket, at our homegoing service.

Get your will together. Talk to key people about what is expected of them and who gets what. A living will and health care power of attorney are important instruments to have in place as well. It is better to be prepared early than to wait one minute too late.

Chapter Seven: Preacher Talk

From every reader, I now turn to preachers more specifically. The following are 11 ideas I want to leave on record for my colleagues - Pastors and preachers:

1. Treat the church right. Because the church is made of people like you and me, it can be one of the most frustrating and even wicked organizations in the world. In the church, the Pastor can pray over and ponder a marvelous plan for God's church. He/she can filter it through seminary education, years of personal experience, and several layers of advisement, just to have it voted down by people who cannot even explain what they are voting down or why they are voting it down.

In the church, you can find people whom you have preached to and taught, prayed for and counseled, and made personal sacrifices for who will believe and give silent consent to unconfirmed rumors about you, spread malicious gossip about you, and withhold their service and giving without even hearing your side of the story. For male Pastors, there is both the temptation of women and money as well as those who will believe a rumor about our being involved with women and misappropriating money.

In the church, you can find people who will suck every ounce of energy out of you, push you beyond all reasonable limits, and not only ask for more but accuse you of being unfit for service. There are some who if you give them 50 hours a week of work, they will ask for 60 hours. If you visit them once or twice in the hospital, they will want you to visit them three of four times. If you go to a high school graduation, they want you to go to an elementary school graduation.

In the church, you can find people who make well over $50,000 a year who give less than $1,000 a year to the church and think it is robbery for the Pastor to be gainfully employed with a growing retirement account. There are those who live in the suburbs and drive luxury vehicles who want the Pastor to live in the ghetto and drive junk cars.

To be clear, the church can be more than frustrating and sometimes wicked. But yet I urge you to treat the church as the bride and body of Christ (see Eph. 5:25-27; Col. 1:24). Love and respect the church, without falling in love. You are not married to the church. The church is Jesus' spouse. Your job is to take care of her on behalf of Jesus.

If you cannot take it anymore, walk, don't run to the exit. Give clear and due notice. Be faithful until your last day. What you say about and do to the church, you say about and do to Jesus. If you love those who mistreat you, God has a way of working things out for your good and doing more with those who have mistreated you than you ever could.

I have seen God promote me, with my sinful self, from one level of grace to the next. I have seen people who have caused me grief suddenly become ill and some even died. Be faithful and trust God to work things out.

2. Preach and teach the verbs. As I will discuss below, formal education has its place. However, church is not Bible college or seminary. The task of the church is not to simply give information and leave people to apply it as best they can. The church is to help people understand relevant information and how to apply it to their lives. As we strive to do this, we must be aware that the way of applying the information for one may not be the same way of applying for the next. For example, the idea of giving your best in service may mean enthusiastic volunteering for the young and broke, while it may mean giving money and using relational influence to recruit volunteers for the older. Being a godly family person may mean being a godly spouse for one and being a godly single aunt/uncle or daughter/son for another.

Original languages, theological constructions, historic reflection, and even social or personal development commentary have their place. However, the core of Pastoral preaching and teaching should be a call to live by the word of God. The aforementioned can be aids but never substitutes.

Be aware that the verbs cause trouble. As the Pharisees became hostile when Jesus' preaching and teaching pointed to their need to repent (i.e., verb), some of the "long standing members" in your church can become hostile about the verbs that God has placed on your heart. John 3:19 talks about people loving darkness, instead of light, because their deeds are evil. Verbless information and stories can be entertaining. Whereas verbs and the call to be doers of the word often leads to hostility. But yet this is what we are called to do. Our preaching and teaching the verbs of God, the call of God, with love will be on the list of things that we will have to answer for as preachers, teachers, and leaders.

3. Get your education, and balance it with experience. I can see the hand of God in my formal education and life experiences. If I had earned my seminary education earlier, I may have been tempted to accept all "White" as right. I may have been tempted to accept as true all of the European theoretical material presented as authoritative and, more damaging, reject all of my Black Baptist heritage and preferences.

If I had went to seminary later in life, I may have been too set in my ways to learn anything. Just as I see people wearing blue jeans with holes in them and sneakers with tears in them because of their comfort, I may have been tempted to do the same with my limited experiences (i.e., more than I already do).

By Pastoring before I went to seminary, I gathered an appreciation for how seminary is not essential for Pastoral ministry. I learned to think without the tutelage of White professors. However, seminary did help me appreciate that the world is much bigger than what is comfortable for my senses and ordinary to my experiences. God is such a big God, and the world is so large that I can be right about my faith and works, while someone else can be right about their faith and works. Just as God called some to be prophets and evangelists, some to be male and others female, some to be hands and others legs, God can work with me in a way different than my fore parents and my other sisters and brothers in Christ.

Seminary taught me that the world is bigger than Black Urban Baptists. My experiences have helped me learn to Pastor Black Baptist churches with some level of effectiveness. Seminary helped me appreciate the forest.

Experience helped me work with the trees at hand.

I urge every preacher to at very least read, make notes, and have discussion with seminarians. But there is no real substitute for the classroom. In the middle are options like online and correspondent schools.

I also urge every preacher to study his/her context, place of ministry, just as diligently as he/she studies the Bible. We are at our best when we bridge the Bible and the people of God that are before us. We are ineffective when we lift our understanding of the Bible and simply call for people to come to our understanding.

4. The first three to five years. I am Pastoring my fourth church. I was at the first church for two years, the second for three years, the third for fourteen years, and the fourth for six years and counting. The first three to five years are the most challenging for me. Not only are you learning the names of people and streets in the city, you don't know who to trust. You are fuzzy about what are the priority issues in the congregation and in the community. And you are even fuzzier about what resources you have at your disposal to deal with priorities, after they are discerned. And yet you are to preach Sunday after Sunday on top of other duties like Bible studies, meeting with officers, meeting with the congregation, hospital calls, funerals, weddings, and counseling.

Consider the following ideas during especially the first five years:

A. Make preaching, teaching, and loving the people your highest priorities. I personally felt led to preach and teach through books of the Bible like Mark, Acts, Titus, Joshua, Judges, Ruth, and so forth. I write teaching notes for Sunday School and Wednesday Bible Study each week as both a guide to my teachers and a resource for my members. I work hard to make sure that all members have a good grasp of the Bible being authoritative truth, salvation being found only in acceptance of Jesus by faith, the call of discipleship (esp., study, serve, and give), and the principles of the local church (e.g., mission, Pastor, members, cabinet, and Christian fellowship).

As for loving the people, I work hard on remembering names, smiling, shaking hands, hugging, being available after worship services and Bible studies to greet the members, and things of this nature. I visit known members in the hospital on a weekly basis, respond to requests to go to the nursing home or a member's home, and monitor reports from my Deacons and Deaconesses regarding those in the nursing home or at home. I give diligence to preaching the eulogy for all of my members as well as for my member's close loved ones, when the service is at the church that I Pastor. I am also rather allowing, if the family wants another clergy person to preach the eulogy.

As for counseling, I am not a certified counselor. However, I am a certified life coach and find coaching much more satisfying to me and helpful to those who want to respond to what is troubling them in a godly way. Counseling tends to look backwards on problems and seek advice from the Pastor. Coaching tends to look forward to goals and seek more facilitation and support than advice from the Pastor.

B. Give diligence to showing the church that you are responsive to their input. I learned to administer an initial and annual church questionnaire at both Macedonia and Southern. In the initial questionnaire, I asked about who is recommended as an advisor to the Pastor and then I asked what are some strengths of the church, weaknesses of the church, and suggestions for improvement in both the initial and annual questionnaires. The advisors proved very helpful, in especially the first few years. They help you interpret the data collected. And they help you gather consensus and support for how to respond to the data.

It is hard for your advisors to openly fight against what they have advised you in doing. For example, if Deacon S. was suggested as an advisor and he advised or supported the plan that is being presented to the church then it will be difficult for him to fight against it, when it gets to the floor. If he does, you may want to find a diplomatic way to help the church understand your confusion about his contradictory advice and lovingly seek agreement with the church. Let it be clearly understood that when you, the Pastor, and the church agree then the meeting is over. Advisors advise; they don't give permission nor do they veto.

Help the church see how you respond to what they say are the strengths, weaknesses, and suggestions for the church. I personally create a document that summarizes the questionnaires and have a session with the church to help them validate the information gathered and understand my intended response. The initial questionnaire may trigger a discussion meeting. The data from the annual questionnaires is incorporated into my annual meeting.

As for the minority who want to talk to you off the record before or after the majority has agreed, remind them that you will listen to them but will respond to the majority's agreement. Don't let influential members or officers get you in a situation where you are following them more than you are following what the majority has said. Fight the temptation of treating some members as if they are more important than others.

C. Give diligence to providing transparent and accountable church leadership. What follows is my system of leadership. My system may not work for you, but I believe that it has been very helpful for me.

On the first and second Sunday of August, I have the annual church questionnaire in the bulletin. I urge all of the members to complete it and turn it in. I compile the information about gender, age, how long they have been a member of the church, their greatest challenges to being a strong disciple of Christ, what they need their church to do to help them with their discipleship, strengths of the church, weaknesses of the church, suggestions for improvement, and anything else they want to share. I create a document that summarizes the largest clusters of data and what I plan on doing in response to the data clusters.

On the last Sunday of August, I have each ministry group to submit their planning material to me for the next year. Planning material includes what the ministry manager thinks are the strengths, weaknesses, and suggestions for improving the ministry group; what the group members think are the strengths, weaknesses, and suggestions for improving the group; three recommendations for who should be the ministry manager for the next year; and recommendations for the group's goals, plans, and budget. As for the recommended ministry manager, by the time you get to the end of year five, this person should be required to come to a Bible study at least monthly, be faithful in a ministry group, and give at least $15/week with a pledge to become a tither.

I review all of the data from the church and the ministry groups with a goal of compiling my first draft of the church's and the ministry department's administrative agendas by the time I get back from the National Baptist Convention, USA, Inc (i.e., early September). An administrative agenda is a document that shows the goals, plans, and budgets for a given year. With the church's administrative agenda, I also have what I call "other leadership items." Here you will find the latest membership roster, the addition of Deacons, a by-law amendment, or anything so significant that I want it to be free standing.

I normally have a monthly Executive Committee Meeting, quarterly Cabinet Meeting, and annual Church Business

Meeting. In September, I meet with my Executive Committee (i.e., ministry superintendents, ministry manager for the Deacons, ministry manager for the Trustees, and the Treasurer). A superintendent is a middle manager between the Pastor and the ministry group. For example, the choirs, ushers, and nurses ministries report to a superintendent who reports to me. A chief goal of the September Executive Committee Meeting is to agree on the church's administrative agenda. They normally have the document for two weeks before I seek their agreement. It is noteworthy that after the Executive Committee's meeting, Executive Committee members can vote "no," but they are not to raise any questions or make any negative comments about what the Pastor is presenting at the Cabinet or Church Meeting.

A chief aim of the October Cabinet Meeting is to agree on the church's administrative agenda. They normally have the document at least two weeks before I seek their agreement. It is noteworthy that after the Cabinet Meeting, Cabinet members can vote "no," but they are not to raise any questions or make any negative comments about what the Pastor is presenting to the church.

And a chief aim of the December Annual Church Business Meeting is to agree on the church's administrative agenda. It is noteworthy that on the first Sunday of November, the church's administrative agenda is made available to the church family. Near the end of November, we will have a discussion meeting. In discussion meetings, any active member outside the Cabinet can ask a question or make a comment for the sake of understanding the material being presented. There will be no vote in the discussion meeting. In early December, we will have our Annual Church Business Meeting, where the active members of the church will be asked to support the Pastor's leadership as presented in the administrative agenda. There will be no questions or comments. The members are to either agree or disagree with what the Pastor is presenting. Every three months I publish a church status report that lets the church know where we are at with each goal and an itemized income and expense statement compared to the agreed upon budget.

In addition to the above, from late September to late October, I meet with the various ministry departments to review and have then sign off showing their understanding and agreeing to carry out their portion of the department administrative agenda.

This system takes time, emotional energy, and strong leadership, but it works for me. Do what works for you. More important than methods is the idea of providing transparent and accountable church leadership.

D. Don't get over extended with community and denominational requests for your participation. It is easy to find yourself in two or three meetings every day with a community group (e.g., NAACP, community council, school board, city council, etc.) or the denomination (i.e., association, state convention, national convention, ministers' conference, etc.). Be clear, these people are calling on you because they assume you have significant influence over your church. This assumption may prove faulty, if you don't invest your first three to five years establishing trust, direction, and routine in your church. Show up at some meetings. Get to know who's who. But be very strategic about your personal commitments.

E. Develop good habits. Don't start stuff that you cannot finish. For example, don't go visit a person in the hospital and call every homebound member every week, if you cannot do the same in year six and beyond. Prayerfully develop a reasonable list of things that you do and realize that no matter what you do, someone will think that it is too little, and someone will think that it is too much. Do those things that give you peaceful conscious. I personally block off 12 hours a week for study (i.e., studying and typing for Sunday School, Wednesday Bible Study, special teachings, Sunday preaching, and special preaching engagements), 16 hours a week for administrative work, I deal with troubled members as they come (3-10 hours/week), in addition to Wednesday evening (and once a month I teach Wednesday noon - 3-5 hours) and Sunday morning (i.e., two preaching services and often a class in between - 7-8 hours).

As important as work is, balance is also important. I take Friday off as much as I can and Saturday, when I can. I take my vacation days. In fact, my wife and I have found great joy in stay-cations (i.e., staying at home and enjoying the city, instead of going somewhere else). Make your health, wealth, and close relationships high priorities. Health includes diet, exercise, sleep, and positive mental attitudes.

I am far from an expert, but I would urge you to at least be open to developing friendships among those outside of your church. You can be friendly, but it will be very difficult to be friends with those in your church. When you have to do something that your friend disagrees with, you may find that your "friend" can turn into an enemy who even tries to cause trouble, by sharing things that you have shared with them in private. But on the other hand, Pastors can be difficult to befriend as well.

5. From year six forward. I would urge you to consider some five year goals for your ministry. And try to aim each year at what you believe to be God's will for the church. Maintain good habits. You should be able to give more to community and denomination, if you have faithful people in place at the church. However, don't become negligent in making sure things are getting done at your church. It may sound harsh, but I believe that it is true: others can do community work, but only the God sent Pastor can Pastor the church.

As for the denomination, until the denomination gets focused on attractive and achievable goals that benefit the churches and broader community with support from the Pastors, I would urge you to be careful about how much time and energy you invest. Pastoring your church is more important than being a Moderator or President of a group that spends more money on hotels and restaurants than it spends on any kind of ministry or mission efforts. Find peaceful conscious between the ideas "you have to be in it to change it" and "some things are just not worth your time."

6. Evangelism. I hold that evangelism is about helping people to accept Christ as their savior by faith. To this end, I have invested great energy in trying to get members to invite and bring their loved ones to church (i.e., worship, study, fellowship activities, etc.) where their loved ones can hear the gospel presented in both a mass presentation, printed material, and by way of designated people who have been trained to present the "Plan of Salvation" to an individual or small group. At the church, visitors are urged to complete visitor cards and sign in for community events (e.g., clothing giveaways, Vacation Bible School, etc.), so a follow up team can call them and try to lead them to Christ or at least back to the church. Almost everyone in the church came because of relational influence, not because of community literature distribution, radio, television, or even internet. Given my experiences, I would urge you to invest 80% of your energy in promoting relational evangelism and 20% in other types of evangelism. My personal evangelism effort is called "Each Reach One."

I must admit that I believe that church would do well to have some events to invite people to come and observe or participate in - side doors into the church. When they come for the Super Bowl party, homeownership conference, start your own business seminar, children's talent show, or whatever you have going on, work on making a great first impression, gathering the contact information, and following up on them.

As you do what you call evangelism, don't forget that church attendance and even membership doesn't equal evangelism. People must accept Jesus as savior by faith, in order to be saved from going to Hell. Make sure you try to measure this and not simply attendance and intake numbers.

7. Discipleship development. By this term, I mean edifying those who have been evangelized. I mean helping people to grow up to be followers of Christ. Three of the elementary measures of discipleship are studying, serving, and giving. I would argue that in order to follow Christ, you must know Him. Bible study is a good way to know Him. As you know and strive to follow Him, you will discover that He wants you to love God with all that you have and to love your neighbor as you love yourself (see Mk. 12:29-31). One way to demonstrate love of others is to be involved in responding to the needs of others, in the name of Jesus. This is called service or ministry. And one way to demonstrate love of God is to stop robbing Him and start trusting Him with your tithes and offerings.

To this elementary list could be added over 1,000 other things like prayer, worship, loving spirit, the fruit of the Spirit, the whole armor of God, and more. However, these things build on studying, serving, and giving. I publish a periodic discipleship roster of those we have a record of studying, serving, and giving at least $10/week. Each month there is a tallying of the number of known disciples. At this writing, we have 212 on our discipleship roster compared to our goal of having 235.

As for methods, I urge you to give quality time and energy in your preaching and teaching to discipleship issues. I have given great effort to developing a culture where people can develop personal discipleship goals and plans as well as accountability relationships with others who have done the same. Our "Discipleship Development Ministry" features a two to four hour orientation course that can be taken independently, personal discipleship goals and plan development, accountability partnership development, and monthly sessions that focus on relevant teachings and sharing.

As I finish this book, I am convicted that a better way to develop disciples may be through what some call "growth groups." A growth group, as I am using the term, is a group of about 12 people who meet weekly for about 90 minutes a session for 10 weeks to share their joys, concerns, prayer, and have a discussion on how to live by a Sunday School lesson, chapter in the Bible, a recent sermon, or any approved curriculum. Find your God given way of developing disciples.

8. Leadership development. The church will only grow so far, if you are the General and everyone else is a Private. Work hard on recruiting and training disciples to be leaders. "Leaders" include ministry managers, teachers, and follow-up workers. It is embarrassing for people to have more training to teach preschoolers than is required to teach God's word in the local church. It is embarrassing to see how much training is required to be a shift leader at McDonalds or a Boy Scout Troop leader compared to how little is required of those who manage ministry in the local church.

We have what I call "Training Union." This is a series of three courses and one of three workshops. Each course and workshop can be taught in four hours or taken independently. The three core and required courses are "Leadership Orientation," "Bible and Doctrine Overview," and "Church and Her Mission." The three workshops are "Management," "Teaching," and "Follow-Up." The workshops include about three months of fieldwork, where a person actually demonstrates that they know how to do what was talked about in the classroom. Most of the ministry work doesn't require Training Union certification.

In addition to filling in the blanks in the books, students are required to quote the following passages of scripture from memory for each course: II Timothy 3:16; II Timothy 2:15; John 3:16; Luke 9:23; and Matthew 28:19-20. There are a series of questions and answers (i.e., catechism) on Bible, salvation, discipleship, giving, and the church that the students are expected to repeat for each class.

The idea is that when the student finishes Training Union, they have a significant familiarity with a body of knowledge that is common to all of the leaders, demonstrated competency in their workshop area, and a track record of studying, serving, and giving as a disciple.

At the time of this writing, we have 62 active Training Union Graduates, which is twice as many as I had at Macedonia. I plan on developing and linking Power Point presentations to our church's website, so students can take the course at their leisure. Find your way of developing leaders.

9. Community and denominational involvement. On one hand, I have so much admiration for people like Dr. Martin Luther King, Jr., Rev. Al Sharpton, Rev. Jessie Jackson, and others. I feel indebted to organizations like the NAACP (i.e., National Association for the Advancement of Colored People), Urban League, SCLC (i.e., Southern Christian Leadership Conference), and others. I don't believe I would have an earned Doctorate degree from a primarily White seminary, if it had not been for a whole army of freedom fighters and advocates. I am also aware that Black churches have played a significant role in racial uplift and community involvement/improvement.

On the other hand, it can be so disheartening to try to work with some of our organizations. The petty bickering, lack of organization, and demand for extra patience and respect are becoming higher hurdles to jump each year for me, not to mention the generation of preachers that is coming along behind me who don't necessarily share my affections or loyalty.

I urge you to find some way to make a contribution to the community outside of your church. This may well mean working in collaboration with existing community groups as well as developing non-profit organizations alongside your church. The world will get darker and more decayed, if we, the light and salt (see Mt. 5:13-16), give up on it.

What I have noted above regarding community involvement can be echoed to a great degree in regard to my beloved Black Baptist denomination. I feel indebted to those who worked so hard before I was even born. However, it is so discouraging to see senior citizens bicker over petty agendas, while priorities like infant mortality, abortion, disproportionate incarceration, the recidivism rate, domestic violence, police and community relations, community violence, and so much more are rarely mentioned and even more rarely acted upon.

I urge you to do what you can do with peaceful conscious to help the sleeping giant of the "Black Baptist Church" to awake and focus on bridging the gaps between the pains of the people and the promises and power of God. In light of the overwhelming majority of those who attend our denominational meetings being over the age of 60, I would urge you work on this area sooner rather than later.

10. Succession planning. Because of the local autonomy of Black Baptist churches, there are some challenges to getting a succession plan in place. In some cases, you may not become comfortable as the Pastor yourself, not to mention trying to set things up for the next person.

I feel good about having a Bible based set of by-laws in place, Pastor search committee guidelines agreed upon by the church, and an Executive Committee who has been trained to keep things afloat at Southern.

One of the greatest compliments to my ministry at Macedonia was that I presided over the selection of the Pastor Search Committee and Moderator before I left. My successor was chosen in about seven months, after my last official day. My successor often commends me for having the church so well prepared to receive their next Pastor.

Do what you can to at least make sure the by-laws are in place, search committee guidelines are in place, a list of supply ministers is handy, and perhaps an interim Pastor is around. If God really blesses you, it would be great to have a co-Pastor or Assistant Pastor who could at least serve as the Pastor for one year after you are gone, after which a search committee can be sent out or he/she can become the Pastor.

I may change my mind before I get there. But at this point, it seems to be God's will for me to give diligence to having a strong Assistant Pastor who will probably become my Co-Pastor when I turn 65 years old. I would hope that we could agree that he/she would become the Acting Pastor for a year, if something happens to me. After that year, the church can decide to send out a search committee or make him/her the Senior Pastor.

11. Write. As you can tell, I am not the greatest writer. However, I think you understand what I am trying to say. It borders on being irresponsible for you to earn a seminary degree, preach and teach for over 20 years, Pastor a church, work in the community, and leave no literary contribution.

I thank God for Charles Spurgeon, Harry Fosdick, and George Buttrick. However, my appreciation for them may be so high because of the rare writings of Black Baptists. If you don't do anything else, do what I have done. Tell the world what God has brought you through to get to where you are. Tell the world about lessons you have learned and aspired to teach others. Leave a collection of sermons, teachings, and or essays behind. To whom much is given much is required (see Lk. 12:48).

Conclusion

It is time to wrap up. I have shared what I consider the major events and developments in my life that have influenced who I am, after 25 years of Pastoring Black Baptists. It should be obvious that I am where I am and do what I do because of God's grace, not because of my own merit. I encourage all readers to seek and obey God's will for your lives. It is getting late in the evening; the sun is going down.

About the Author

Rev. Dr. Robert E. Baines, Jr. has served as a Senior Pastor since 1990. The Southern Baptist Church, in Cincinnati, Ohio, is where he currently serves. His Doctorate of Ministry Degree was earned at the United Theological Seminary, in Trotwood, Ohio.

He believes that what he lacks in grammar is compensated for with practical Bible based wisdom. ***Please note that a portion of his book profits benefit youth programming; charitable causes like prostate cancer, breast cancer, and MS research; and disaster relief.***

Here are some other books that he has recently written,

Dealing With Difficult People: 31 Empowering Christian Devotionals For Those Dealing With Negative, Manipulative, or Mean People (Dealing With Difficult People Series, Volume 4)

Mean People: A Step-by-Step Christian Plan for Dealing With Mean and Nasty People

(Dealing With Difficult People Series, Volume 3)

Manipulative People: A Step-by-Step Christian Plan for Dealing With Liars and Controlling People (Dealing With Difficult People Series, Volume 2)

Negative People: A Step-by-Step Christian Plan for Dealing With Complaining Emotional Vampires (Dealing With Difficult People Series, Volume 1)

How to Deal With Guilt: A Step-By-Step Christian Plan for Dealing With Guilt and Feeling Guilty (Negative Emotions Series, Volume One)

Inspiration From Psalm 23: Life Changing Messages, 23 Devotionals, and 6 Live Sermons

See all of my books at
www.RobertBaines.org

Made in the USA
Middletown, DE
08 September 2019